A ROOKIE BIOGRAPHY

EWIS CARROLL

thor of Alice in Wonderland

By Carol Greene

CHILDRENS PRESS®

CHICAGO

This book is for Julia Bullock.

Lewis Carroll (Charles Dodgson) 1832-1898

Library of Congress Cataloging-in-Publication Data

Greene, Carol.
    Lewis Carroll, author of the Alice books / by Carol Greene.
       p. cm. — (A Rookie biography)
    Summary: A brief biography of the nineteenth-century British
mathematician, teacher, photographer, and author, best known for his
"Alice" books.
    ISBN 0-516-04227-0
    1. Carroll, Lewis, 1832-1898—Biography—Juvenile literature.
2. Authors, English—19th century—Biography—Juvenile literature.
[1. Carroll, Lewis, 1832-1898. 2. Authors, English.] I. Title. II. Series:
Greene, Carol. Rookie biography.
PR4612.G74 1992
828'.809—dc20   91-37821
                                      CIP
                                       AC

Lewis Carroll was
a real person.
His actual name was
Charles Lutwidge Dodgson.
He lived from 1832 to 1898
and wrote stories about
a little girl called Alice.
This is his story.

TABLE OF CONTENTS

Chapter 1

"Please Explain"

Young Charlie Dodgson took
a math book to his father.

"Please explain," said Charlie.

"You are much too young
for these hard problems,"
said his father.

Charlie nodded.
He knew the problems were hard.

"*But*," he said, "please explain."

Charlie liked to think.
He liked to figure things out
and make things up.

When he was older, he
made up games and stories
for his 10 sisters and brothers.
He even made up games
for toads, snails, and worms.
Charlie liked animals, too.

Charlie liked to play
with all kinds of animals.

Charlie's father was a clergyman
in the Church of England.
At first he had a church
far out in the country.
Then he moved to one in Croft
and the family lived in town.

Charlie built a train that
ran around their new garden.
He made it from a wheelbarrow,
a barrel, and a dolly—
a platform on wheels.

He also made a theater
with marionettes for actors.
Then he wrote plays
and put them on for his family.

Charlie wrote magazines
for his family, too.
Often they were funny.
He wrote such silly verses as:

"Drink tea, not coffee.
Never eat toffy.
Eat bread with butter.
Once more, don't stutter."

Charlie didn't really think
stuttering was funny.
He stuttered and had
trouble hearing, too.
These things bothered
him all his life.

When he was 12, Charlie
went away to Richmond School.
He did very well there.

Boys playing a ball game called cricket at Rugby School.

"Don't tell Charles," wrote
the head of the school
to Charlie's father.
"But he is much smarter
than the other boys."

When he was almost 14,
Charlie went to Rugby School.
Some boys there were cruel.
Charlie didn't like that.

At last he came home and spent
a year studying for college.
He had time to figure things out
and make things up.
Charlie was happy again.

Charles Dodgson
graduated from
Oxford University
(below). Later he
taught mathematics
at Christ Church
College in
Oxford University.

Chapter 2

" 'Twas Brillig"

Charles Dodgson had just arrived
at Oxford University when
something sad happened.
His mother died.

Charles hurried home
for her funeral.
Then he went back to school.
But he never stopped
missing his beloved mother.

Charles worked hard at Oxford.
He won many prizes in math.
In 1856, he began to
teach math at Oxford.

Some people thought
Charles was unfriendly.
But that wasn't true.
His stuttering and his poor
hearing just made him quiet.

Charles Dodgson
at age 25

Boat races were popular at Oxford.

Charles liked to go out
with his friends.
He liked rowing on the river
and seeing plays in London.
He still liked writing, too.

He wrote some poems for
a magazine, *The Train*.
The head of the magazine
thought Charles should use
a different name for his writing.

So Charles made up some names.
The man chose "Lewis Carroll."
Some people knew that
Lewis Carroll was really Charles.
But not everyone did.
Charles liked to keep it a secret.

One day, when Charles was
feeling silly, he wrote
part of a silly poem.

Charles drew
this picture
of himself
and called it
"What I look
like when I'm
lecturing."

"'Twas brillig and the slithy toves
Did gyre and gimble in the wabe."

No one knew what it meant,
not even Charles.
But one day, people everywhere
would love that silly poem.

People who had their picture taken with the old
cameras had to stay very still for a long time.

Charles found a new hobby, too.
Back then, cameras were
huge and hard to work.
But Charles got one
and practiced until he
could take very good pictures.

Then one day, Charles' boss said
Charles must become a clergyman
in the Church of England
if he wanted to go on
living at Oxford University.

Charles didn't want to be
a priest like his father.
But he loved God and
knew a lot about religion.
So in 1861, he became a deacon.

"I can stay here and
serve God by teaching
and writing," he thought.

That turned out to be
a good choice for Charles.

Chapter 3

"The Tale of Wonderland"

Charles always liked children.
He could relax with them.
They didn't care about his
stuttering or his hearing.

He took pictures of children,
wrote them funny letters,
and told them funny stories.

Charles took this photograph of the Liddell sisters.

Charles' favorite children
were the Liddell sisters—
Lorina, Alice, and Edith.
Their father was the dean
of Christ Church of
Oxford University.

Rowing on the river

July 4, 1862, turned out to be
a special day for all children.
On that day, Charles and
his friend, Robinson Duckworth,
took the Liddell girls
on a boat trip up the river.

As he rowed, Charles began
to tell the girls a story.
It was about a little girl
called Alice who fell
down a rabbit hole.

Opposite page: Alice meets the Cheshire Cat and the Queen of Hearts (inset).
Above: Alice at a tea party with the Mad Hatter, a rabbit, and a dormouse

There, in a different land,
she met a White Rabbit,
the Cheshire Cat, the Dormouse,
the Mad Hatter, the Queen of Hearts,
and many other strange folks.

"Curiouser and curiouser!"
said Alice in the story.

When the day was over,
Alice Liddell said,
"Oh, Mr. Dodgson, please
write out the story for me."

Charles did.
Then he found a company
to turn his story into a book.
They called the book
Alice's Adventures in Wonderland.

"I will use my other name,
Lewis Carroll," said Charles.
"And make the cover red, please."

Chapter 1

Alice was beginning to get very tired of sitting by her sister on the bank, and of having nothing to do: once or twice she had peeped into the book her sister was reading, but it had no pictures or conversations in it, and where is the use of a book, thought Alice, without pictures or conversations? So she was considering in her own mind, (as well as she could, for the hot day made her feel very sleepy and stupid,) whether the pleasure of making a daisy-chain was worth the trouble of getting up and picking the daisies, when a white rabbit with pink eyes ran close by her.

There was nothing very remarkable in that, nor did Alice think it so very much out of the way to hear the rabbit say to itself "dear, dear!" ... she thought it over afterwards ... she ought to ... it all ...

The first pages of _Alice's Adventures in Wonderland_

A Christmas Gift to a Dear Child in Memory of a Summer Day.

dried her eyes to see what was coming. It was the white rabbit coming back again, splendidly dressed, with a pair of white kid gloves in one hand, and a nosegay in the other. Alice was ready to ask help of any one, she felt so desperate, and as the rabbit passed her, she said, in a low, timid voice, "If you please, Sir —" the rabbit started violently, looked up once into the roof of the hall, from which the voice seemed to come, and then dropped the nosegay and the white kid gloves, and skurried away into the darkness as hard as it could go.

Alice took up the nosegay and gloves, and found the nosegay so delicious that she kept smelling at it all the time she went on talking to herself — "dear, dear how queer everything is today! and yesterday everything happened just as usual: I wonder if I was changed in the night? Let me think: was I the same when I got up this morning? I ...

John Tenniel

1889

A man called John Tenniel
drew pictures for the book.
It came out on June 27, 1865.
Thousands of people
bought it for their children.
The children loved it.

Charles called that trip on the river with the Liddells "a golden afternoon." He wrote a poem about it for the start of the book. Part of that poem goes:

"Thus grew the tale of Wonderland:
Thus slowly, one by one,
Its quaint events were hammered out—
And now the tale is done,
And home we steer, a merry crew,
Beneath the setting sun."

"Lewis Carroll" telling stories to his young friends

Chapter 4

More *Alice* and the *Snark*

While children read *Alice,*
Charles went on teaching math,
taking photos, and seeing plays.

In 1867, he went to Russia.
It was a long trip,
and Charles got homesick.
He never went so far again.

It was a lot more fun,
he decided, to invite
his young friends to dinner.
The children liked that, too.

They could listen to
Charles' 14 music boxes.
They could play with his dolls
and his wind-up bear.
They could dress up in costumes
and he'd take their picture.

Charles also told them riddles
and jokes and stories and
gave them a fine dinner.

Alice Liddell
was Charles
Dodgson's
favorite child.
He wrote
about her
in his most
famous books.

He was writing more books, too.
Most were about math.
But he had an idea for
a new book about Alice,
and at last he wrote it.

33

John Tenniel drew these pictures
for *Through the Looking Glass*
In this book, Alice walks
through a mirror into
Looking-Glass House. Later, she
meets Tweedledum and Tweedledee (above).
Opposite page: Alice meets
Humpty Dumpty and two queens
in *Through the Looking Glass*.

In this book, Alice goes
through a mirror to a new land.
She meets talking flowers,
chess people, Humpty Dumpty,
Tweedledum, and Tweedledee.

Alice also finds a book.
In it is a poem called
"Jabberwocky" that starts:

"'Twas brillig and the slithy toves
Did gyre and gimble in the wabe."

At last Charles had found
a place for that silly poem.

Through the Looking Glass
came out on December 6, 1871.
Children loved it, too.

Then Charles went back
to his math books.
But one day, as he walked
near his sisters' home,
a sentence popped into his head.

"For the Snark *was*
a Boojum, you see."

Charles didn't know
what that sentence meant.
But he sat down and wrote
a long poem to go with it.
Out came another book,
The Hunting of the Snark.

Cover and pictures
from the long poem
The Hunting of the Snark

Much later, some children
wrote to Charles and asked
what the Snark poem meant.

"I'm very much afraid
I didn't mean anything
but nonsense!" wrote Charles.

39

Charles Dodgson (left)
worked in this
room (above) at
Christ Church, Oxford.

Chapter 5

"So Kind"

Later, Charles wrote
Sylvie and Bruno and
Sylvie and Bruno Concluded.
Parts of the books were funny,
but children liked
the *Alice* stories better.

Charles went on working
at Oxford University
for the rest of his life.
Much of the time,
he had to be serious.

But he still thought
about silly things, too,
like a man whose feet
were so big that he had to
put his pants on over his head.

Part of Charles wanted
to be a child forever.
That's why he liked children
and making up silly things
and being Lewis Carroll.

On January 14, 1898,
when Charles was almost 66,
he died at his sisters' home.

Children everywhere cried.
They decided to send money for
a bed in a children's hospital.
It would be called the
Alice in Wonderland bed.

Years later, people
gave money for a whole
children's ward at a hospital,
the Lewis Carroll ward.

Many adults could never
understand Charles Dodgson.
But his young friends did.

"What was he really like?"
people would ask them.
And the children all
said the same thing.
"He was so kind!"

Important Dates

1832   January 27—Born at Daresbury, Cheshire, England, to Charles and Frances Dodgson

1843   Family moved to Croft, Yorkshire

1844   Entered Richmond School

1846   Entered Rugby School

1851   Went to Christ Church College, Oxford University

1856   Became lecturer in math, Christ Church College

1861   Ordained deacon (officer) in Church of England

1862   Told story of Alice to Liddell sisters

1865   *Alice's Adventures in Wonderland* published

1871   *Through the Looking Glass* published

1876   *The Hunting of the Snark* published

1898   January 14—Died at Guildford, England

INDEX

Page numbers in boldface type indicate illustrations.

PHOTO CREDITS

ABOUT THE AUTHOR

Carol Greene has degrees in English literature and musicology. She has worked in international exchange programs, as an editor, and as a teacher of writing. She now lives in Webster Groves, Missouri, and writes full-time. She has published more than 100 books, including those in the Childrens Press Rookie Biographies series.